An ironmonger at his stall in Reading, Berkshire, in the 1890s.

THE VICTORIAN IRONMONGER

Cecil A. Meadows

Shire Publications

CONTENTS

ACKNOWLEDGEMENTS
The publishers acknowledge with gratitude the receipt of information from Mr P. F. G. Littlewood, Projects Manager, Robert Dyas Ltd. They also express their thanks to the owners of the copyright of the various advertisements and items from trade catalogues that have been reproduced, particularly to the editor of the *Hardware Trade Journal*. Photographs are acknowledged as follows: Robert Dyas Ltd, page 14; Halliwell's House Museum, Selkirk, page 32; Science Museum, London, pages 16 and 20 (top two). The key trade sign on page 5 is reproduced by courtesy of Eleanor Harrison (photograph Mike Bass).

Cover: *Blyth's ironmongery stores (see page 3).*

British Library Cataloguing in Publication Data: Meadows, Cecil A. (Cecil Austen). The Victorian ironmonger. – 3rd ed. – (A Shire album; no. 32) 1. Hardware stores – Great Britain – History – 19th century I. Title 338.4'7'683'0941'09034. ISBN 0 7478 0456 7.

Published in 2008 by Shire Publications Ltd, Midland House, West Way, Botley, Oxford OX2 0PH, UK. (Website: www.shirebooks.co.uk)
Copyright © 1978, 1984 and 2003 by the estate of Cecil A. Meadows. First published 1978. Second edition 1984; reprinted 1986, 1992 and 1997. Third edition 2000; reprinted 2003 and 2008. Shire Album 32. ISBN 978 0 7478 0456 7.
Cecil A. Meadows is hereby identified as the author of this work in accordance with Section 77 of the Copyright, Designs and Patents Act 1988.

Printed in Great Britain by Ashford Colour Press Ltd, Unit 600, Fareham Reach, Fareham Road, Gosport, Hampshire PO13 0FW.

The premises of Blyth, ironmonger, in North Walsham, Norfolk, about 1900. Note the extensive stock of oil lamps in the window.

INTRODUCTION

Until about 1960 it was possible to find ironmongers' shops that hinted at the former glory of the trade and conveyed a feeling of confidence that all needs could be supplied. There we would be conditioned to hope for a larger range of screws, old latches and old-fashioned items of ironmongery. In their Victorian heyday such shops might well have provided the bulk of our household goods, indoor and outdoor, with a large range to choose from. The large furnishing and general ironmongers were the domestic department stores. In addition they would expect to make, install, modify, maintain and repair many items.

The writer was apprenticed, in the late 1920s, to one of the last of such ironmongers trading in Norwich. The aftermath of the upheaval of the First World War had seen the closure of many competitors: his firm, founded in 1797, had survived because it had diversified into large-scale wholesaling and the trade distribution of cycles, motorcycles and motorcar accessories. The manufacturing side, devoted largely to tin and japanned ware, was operating on a much reduced scale, and supplies were supplemented and replaced by mass-produced items. The era of the furnishing ironmonger was almost at an end.

ORIGINS OF THE NAME AND TRADE

Middle English spellings of the word *ironmonger* include *yrenmongere, yrinmonger* and *irenmonger,* and in the thirteenth century the terms *le ferun, le ferur* and *le ferronius,* derived from Latin, were still in use. *Hardware,* meaning ironmongery or small goods or wares of metal, is a term which was first used in about 1515.

The word *ironmonger* is unknown in the United States of America, and *hardwareman* is the title that has become official in Britain since the National Federation of Ironmongers changed its name to the British Hardware Federation, a change resisted by many members. The trade magazine is called *Hardware Today.*

Early maps of towns show that most trading was done at booths or stalls in the market place, grouped together by trades. For instance, in thirteenth-century Norwich there were three ironmongers side by side in Ironmonger Row and they sold nails, iron for the smiths, cart tyres and horseshoes. As far back as the reign of Edward I (1272–1307) the ironmongers were established in the Cheapside area of London; later they moved to Fenchurch Street so that they would be nearer the river where their forges would cause less of a nuisance.

The Worshipful Company of Ironmongers, one of the twelve great City guilds, was founded before 1348 and incorporated in 1463. Later it adopted St Lawrence as its patron saint, depicted holding a gridiron, the emblem of his martyrdom. The government of the Ironmongers' Company consists of the whole body of the Livery, an unusual arrangement, and a body of freemen called the Yeomanry.

The arms of the Worshipful Company are blazoned as follows: 'argent, on a chevron gules, three swivels or (the central one palewise, the other two in the line of the ordinary), between as many steel gads azure'. The old motto *Assher dure* means roughly that steel lasts, and appropriately the supporters are salamanders.

This advertisement appeared in 1850. Cubitt not only manufactured thrashing machines but sold fire irons and cutlery as well.

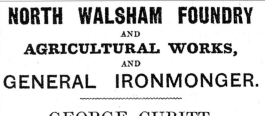

TRADE SIGNS

Traders' signs, a prominent feature of streets in the seventeenth and eighteenth centuries, were still widespread when Queen Victoria came to the throne in 1837. They survived well into the twentieth century, and today many of them can be seen in museums.

A golden key was the most popular sign for an ironmonger: it provided such a direct reminder of his occupation that it required no explanation. Generally made of wood, the key would be highly decorated and gilded. The padlock was next in popularity, and fine specimens still exist. Domestic items – the gridiron, frying pan, dustpan, tea kettle, candlestick and ewer – were all used as signs in Victorian times. The tool side of the trade was signified by hand saws, circular saws, planes, ploughshares and ploughs, a few of which survived in rural areas into the mid twentieth century. One Norwich ironmonger, who was also a tobacconist, had as his sign a golden pipe, a churchwarden type made of iron and gilded. This sign disappeared after the First World War when the three-hundred-year old firm ceased trading.

Trade signs were widely used on the invoices and letter-headings of the Victorians and provide evidence for historians where the actual signs have vanished.

Above: *This ironmonger's trade sign is 23 inches (58 cm) long and weighs 4 pounds (1.8 kg).*

Left: *In 1850 Howlett & Company advertised papier mâché trays, table mangles, Budding's grass cutter and the Somapantic Bath.*

The interior of Theobald, Johnson & Burton, ironmongers, in London Street, Norwich, in 1893. Note the display of tennis racquets.

THE GROWTH AND DECLINE OF THE FURNISHING IRONMONGER

During the Victorian period the great furnishing ironmongery businesses rose to prominence and began their decline. They were virtually departmental stores, taking every new invention in their stride – gas lighting and cooking, cycles, motorcycles and even cars, electrical apparatus, gramophones, typewriters and sports goods. They were aggressive and far-sighted traders.

They were able to undertake the necessary repairs in their existing workshops, for they were practical people, able to master technical complexities. Well into the twentieth century many ironmongers sold and repaired items like cycles, electrical and sports goods, but on the whole specialists took from the ironmonger the trades that he had initiated and fostered. By the end of Victoria's reign there were sports dealers who were able to serve all the needs of the sporting and leisure-seeking public, cycle dealers who could cater for every need of the growing army of cyclists, electrical dealers who confined themselves to the sale and promotion of all things

No. 666/36 VILLA RAILING AND GATE.

From a trade catalogue of builders' sundries, 1899.

electric, and china shops, music shops and big departmental stores.

At the end of the nineteenth century the ironmonger continued to offer a wide range of merchandise, but greater changes were on the way. The trend in both supply and demand was towards equipment that was smaller and easier to handle, in order to fit in with changes in lifestyle. Suburbia, with its thousands of new small dwellings, produced a market for household apparatus like small carpet-sweepers, light portable wringers and washing machines. The increase in cooking by gas led to a demand for lighter pans, which were made of new steel enamelled ware, and aluminium kitchenware was about to appear. Household gadgets and simple appliances were flooding in from the United States and the Continent. Small, neat gardens called for a range of simpler, lighter tools and gadgets. Electric light joined gas in ousting the oil lamp. The monumental style of the old ironmongers was out of date, and in the evolution towards our modern way of life, accelerated by the upheaval of the First World War, the scale of business contracted and the old grandeur faded gradually away.

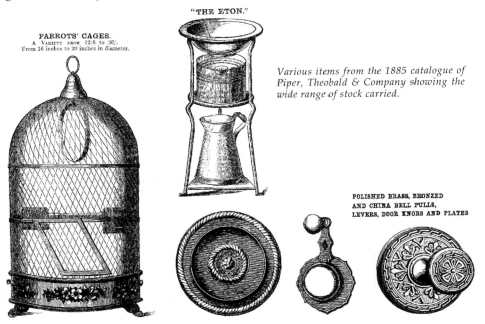

"THE ETON."

PARROTS' CAGES.
A Variety from 12/6 to 30/-.
From 16 inches to 20 inches in diameter.

Various items from the 1885 catalogue of Piper, Theobald & Company showing the wide range of stock carried.

POLISHED BRASS, BRONZED
AND CHINA BELL PULLS,
LEVERS, DOOR KNOBS AND PLATES

SUPPLIES AND INVENTIONS

The manufacturers who relied on the ironmongers for distribution were bold and competitive, quick to exploit the improving technology and unique inventiveness of the time. Eager though they were to sell and make profits, they were equally keen to produce worthy goods of recognised quality. Approval for their products was sought in competition at exhibitions where medals were awarded for excellence. The Great Exhibition of 1851 in Hyde Park was followed by a succession of national and international exhibitions displaying the latest and best the world was producing. The gold, silver and bronze medallists in each class proudly announced their success on all their stationery.

At Hyde Park in 1851 many of the wares to be retailed by the ironmongers were exhibited by firms well on the way to the ascendancy they still have, though not always in the same lines. In the china, porcelain and earthenware section were H. Minton & Company with terracotta and tableware, W. T. Copeland & Company with porcelain statuary vases, china, earthenware, cut and engraved glass, and Wedgwood & Sons with Jasper ware, Queensware, statuary and terracotta.

The furniture section showed novelties like an invalid washstand, a stove that could bake, roast, boil, fry and heat plates all at the same time, machine-made paper hangings and washable wallpapers.

The Sheffield section had saws by Spear & Jackson, carpenters' tools by R. Marples and a range of knives, including the Prince of Wales' Sailor's Knife by Thomas Turner & Company. Joseph Rodgers & Sons triumphed with a specially made sportsman's knife with seventy-five blades. Chubb & Son exhibited fireproof safes and patent detector locks.

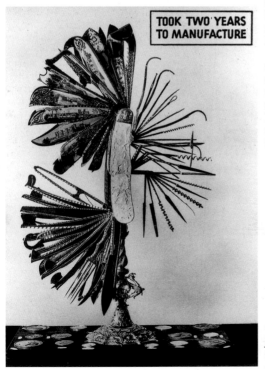

TOOK TWO YEARS TO MANUFACTURE

Ten years later Shanks of Arbroath exhibited lawn-mowers, Ransomes of Ipswich steam engines and thrashing machines, W. & T. Avery scales, W. Wilkinson & Son shears, Kilner Brothers glass bottles and jars, the Coalbrookdale Company cast-iron wares.

The Norfolk Knife, which contained seventy-five blades, was made for the Great Exhibition of 1851 by the Sheffield cutlers Joseph Rodgers & Sons Ltd.

This early gas cooker from the Rothschilds' London mansion was made by Alfred King of Liverpool, 1859.

New lines and improved methods and materials did not necessarily replace established stocks: the natural conservatism of both retailers and the public required that items were initially additions not replacements. Any major development had also to be understood and accepted by the ironmonger as he had to introduce and perhaps install and maintain it. Nevertheless stocks expanded steadily as the ironmonger undertook the sale of a diverse range of goods.

A few of the products invented or discovered between 1830 and 1850 are corrugated iron (1832), creosote (1833), emery paper (1843), the safety razor (1847), the vapour compression refrigerator (1845), the knife-cleaning machine (1844), the screw thread (1847) and the wood screw (1845). In the latter half of the century appeared the revolving cowl (1850), paraffin from shale (1856), the Duplex paraffin burner (1865), the gas geyser (1865), the gas cooker (1865), the gas fire (1880), the washdown closet (1870), the sewing machine (1829 – Singer 1850), wire netting, carborundum (1891), aluminium (1886), celluloid (1860) and the phonograph (1877).

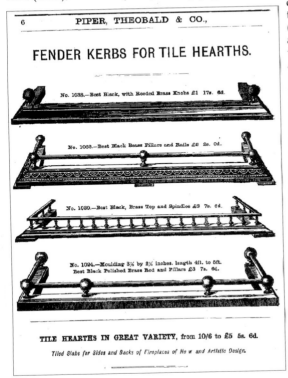

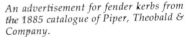

An advertisement for fender kerbs from the 1885 catalogue of Piper, Theobald & Company.

An ironmongery warehouse in Castle Street, Norwich, 1900.

PURCHASING METHODS

Although there was such a marked increase in trading activity, the purchasing methods of the Victorians seem absurdly simple by present-day standards. Prices were remarkably stable over long periods. Buyers used their own judgement as to the suitability and quality of the merchandise for there was no advertising pressure to force the stocking of certain brands. Where there was a traditional conservative attitude, new products did not always reach the shelves as quickly as they do today. A good example of this was the reluctance to stock enamelled ware when it made its appearance; tinware, copperware and cast iron were all said to be superior, but the eventual mass-production of enamelled ware, with its price and colour range, won the battle.

From the middle of the nineteenth century the manufacturers issued elaborate catalogues, often expensively bound and remaining current for years, apart from the infrequent insertion of revision slips and new products. The ironmonger bought direct from the manufacturer, until the large wholesale houses grew up towards the end of the period.

The rapid growth of the railways ensured the swift delivery of goods from the works, a great improvement on the previous slow delivery by water or road wagon. The larger rural ironmongers acted as local wholesalers, and many employed travellers to call on the small traders and village shops in their locality. In turn the larger ironmongers published extensive catalogues of their stock ranges.

Nº0024

Nº0019

Nº007

Nº0021

Height 2ft 1in Width 14in

Height 2ft 5in Width 15¾in

Height 2ft in Width 18in

Height 2ft 7½in Width 16½in

Part of a range of cast-iron umbrella stands, from a manufacturer's catalogue of the 1890s.

Some of the travellers from the manufacturers were partners or even proprietors, particularly in the iron and tool trades, and their regular visits resulted in lifelong friendships, ensuring a continuity of supplies. The accounts were usually journey accounts subject to a settlement discount when the traveller arrived, even if the intervals were as great as six months: long credit was normal practice, and the discounts seem unusually generous by present-day standards.

An advertisement from 'The Ironmonger' in the 1880s.

Commercial travelling in Victorian times: Mr G. J. Burton, a Norwich ironmonger, on his rounds.

TRADING AND DELIVERY

Although horse-drawn vehicles were the order of the day, deliveries were prompt in the cities and large centres and many traders prided themselves on their same-day delivery service.

In the rural areas, goods were delivered by the national network of carriers' carts, privately owned and each serving a clearly defined and restricted area. Some inns and taverns catered specially for this trade. The carriers brought orders to the shops in the morning for execution the same day and they left the city between four and five o'clock, delivering all the way as they went home, usually a maximum of 20 miles (32 km).

Shop hours were long, starting generally at eight and finishing at six to seven o'clock, with no half day, only a slightly earlier finish on a particular day. Tea breaks were not the organised function of today; in the ironmongery trade frequent clandestine trips to the public house around the corner were the custom. A public house in Norwich named the Ironmongers' Arms, the only one so called in Britain, owed its name to the patronage of nearby members of the trade. Though the shops were heated in a meagre way, the stockrooms were not, except for the odd small heater – hard conditions when handling cold ironware in the winter. The traditional garb was a black apron, a cap and old heavy-duty clothing for the humping of such items as prickly bags of nails weighing a hundredweight (50 kg) or cumbersome reels of barbed wire, both very destructive of clothing.

Stockrooms were vast and rambling, and the heavy items as well as nails and oils were kept in the cellars. Here nails were wrapped up in smaller parcels, say 7 or 14 pounds (3.2 or 6.4 kg), done so neatly as to resemble a wrapped house brick. Paints were mixed to order, generally in a small paint mill, from the paste ingredients in stock.

The shops were not brightly lit; even the main shops with their large hanging oil lamps would seem very dingy by present electrical standards. The floors were bare boards constantly swept clean with damp sawdust.

The whole tempo of selling was slow. Ironmongery did not lend itself to speed as most of the stock was not on show but kept in stockrooms, often quite remote from the shop. The ironmonger's shop had a highly distinctive smell with a strong basis of paraffin, glue, oils and general drysaltery.

Grave crosses were one of the more sombre stock lines of the Victorian ironmonger.

PRICE CODES AND STOCK MARKING

Victorian ironmongers were most punctilious in the price marking of their stock, and in an era of stable prices firm marking was possible. Most items were marked in ink from the familiar brown stone bottle of Henry Stephens, a sharpened stick serving as a pen.

Tinware was rubbed on the marking spot with a little whiting so that the ink did not retreat, and there were traditional marking spots varying from firm to firm. Large tools, heavy items and cast-iron ware were marked with white paint, generally a mixture of white lead and turpentine.

Normally the mark showed the invoice number, the cost price and both wholesale and retail prices. These were in the private code of the firm; plain figures were rarely used, so that the seller had as much room to manoeuvre as he thought fit. This flexibility was particularly necessary in the rural areas, where every sale involved much hard bargaining.

The selling codes, indicating retail price, were letter-based, and the following are actual examples from East Anglian businesses.

1	2	3	4	5	6	7	8	9	0
G	O	D	W	I	T	H	U	S	Z

1	2	3	4	5	6	7	8	9	10	11
C	H	E	K	D	A	P	R	O	N	S

1	2	3	4	5	6	7	8	9	10
C	U	M	B	E	R	L	A	N	D

Cost codes were often based on the square. The one below left was so familiar to the writer that he could quite easily add, subtract and divide in it, often in his head.

Where discounts were obtained from these costs they were shown as in the example below right:

1	2	3	4	5	6	7	8	9
˥	⊂	⊤	⊣	⊦	+	˩	∠	⊥

10	11	12	13	14	15	16	17	18

5% 7½% 10% 12½% 15%

17½% 20% 25% 30%.

Combinations such as 50 per cent, which equalled two of twenty-five per cent, would be shown thus:

The shop of Tily & Brown in Castle Street, Farnham, Surrey, photographed in the early years of the twentieth century.

THE OFFICE

In the early days of the Victorian era the ironmonger had to cope with none of the legislation that preoccupies his present-day counterpart: his office dealt only with book-keeping and trade correspondence.

The industrial acts affecting his operations, such as the Employers' Liability Act (1880), the Workmen's Compensation Act (1897) and the Factory Workshop Acts (1878 and 1895), were of late Victorian origin.

There was no PAYE, and income tax, which was by present-day standards merely a nominal amount, did not apply to the majority of the staff. Many employers kept their wages records in small pocket books, kept personally by the owner, and boys were referred to as 'boy' without a name.

The office layout remained unchanged for years, furnished with tall box-like desks with sloping tops and lift-up lids; the clerks, mainly male, perched on tall stools in Dickensian style.

A large amount of business was done on credit; certainly the nobility expected and took it, and many accounts were rendered only annually. In the shop the entries were written straight into a long day book, which was posted weekly into the ledger. The cashier in the office was generally one of the partners, the taking of money being of supreme importance and requiring discretion when discounts were asked for.

MANUFACTURING

The Victorian ironmonger was essentially a practical man and the workshop was a most important part of his business. Apart from the installation of coal-fired ranges and grates and hot-water systems, there was gas-fitting and bell-fitting (the pull-crank type), a highly skilled trade. In the larger houses miles of wire and hundreds of fittings were used. Tinware, copper and japanned wares and many items such as saucepans and kettles were made on the premises. In the case of kettles the spouts, lids and knobs were bought in.

The larger businesses, especially in rural areas, usually had a small foundry attached which produced a wide variety of castings, particularly for agricultural implements. In some cases the foundry prospered to such a degree that it became the main activity and the retail shop was hived off or closed down.

Many large national firms grew out of retail ironmongery. Boulton & Paul Ltd of Norwich sold their retail shop in 1869 to a neighbouring firm and concentrated, in new works, on manufacturing wire netting and cast-iron products such as lawn-mowers, grates and ranges. Similarly, Barnard, Bishop & Barnard, the inventors of woven wire netting, gave up their retail ironmongery shop in Norwich and devoted themselves to wire netting, castings, wire products, wrought ironwork and material for rural estates. Becoming known as Barnards, they were taken over after the Second World War by Tinsley Wire Industries. Their original wire-netting machine is in the Bridewell Museum in Norwich.

TOILET SETS from 13/6 to 40/ per set.

Papier Mache Trays, from 25/ to 105/ per set.

Canton Jugs, from 2/3

Japanned Trays, from 7/6 to 35/ per set.

Parisian Jugs, in Zinc or Brass, from 2/

Japanned Coal Vases, from 6/ to 40/

Hot Water Cans, from 2/

A selection of goods available from Piper, Theobald & Company in Norwich, taken from their 1885 catalogue.

THE STOCKS

Considering the wide range of stocks, it is hard to believe the Victorian ironmonger could find room for all of it and it is easy to understand the growth of specialist traders at the end of the nineteenth century and the contraction of many businesses after the First World War.

Many of the builders' merchants of the twentieth century grew out of the special department where tradesmen would buy sanitary ware and builders' ironmongery – rainwater goods, locks and fittings, plumbers' supplies and roofing materials, even basic building materials. The sale of tools was very important for tradesmen such as builders, carpenters, wheelwrights, engineers, coachbuilders, smiths and gardeners. The range was far greater than can be found today, except for very good specialist shops.

Early in the period nails were mainly wrought and hand-made until the machine-made, cut-steel varieties appeared. Wire nails were known as French nails and were commonly called by their price per hundred: twopenny (1 inch or 254 mm), sixpenny (2 inches or 508 mm) to tenpenny ($2^3/4$ inches or 699 mm) and twelvepenny (3 inches or 762 mm). Nettleford & Chamberlain introduced the patent wood screw to Britain in 1845 and supplied vast quantities of these and of nails, nuts and bolts.

An early wooden gas cooker, c.1850, now in the Science Museum, London.

Paint consisted mainly of dry colours and paste in oil or turpentine for the tradesman or supplier to mix, although there was a limited range of ready-mixed oil paints in sombre colours. Red and white lead, spirits of turpentine and linseed oil were all standard stock. Wallpapers began to be popular, starting at $1^1/2$d a roll, though at this level the colours were strong and crude; the subdued range known as sanitary papers were often dark and rather depressing, to match the ready-mixed paint. Linoleum, also in stock, added the final gloomy touch in many cases; coconut-fibre matting was a little more cheerful.

The Victorian ironmonger supplied all forms of lighting. His cellar would contain Russian tallow, Stockholm tar, paraffin, colza, cod and sperm oils, linseed oil and turpentine, quantities changing as the century wore on. In country districts paraffin predominated from the mid-nineteenth-century development of paraffin burners (particularly the invention of the twin-wick Duplex burner in 1865) until the spread of electricity in the 1920s and 1930s. There was a huge trade in glass chimneys and globes. In towns gas became the principal illuminant even though the mantles that transformed the quality of light produced did not appear until the end of the century. The ironmonger installed, serviced and supplied all the fittings and kept constant stocks of Bijou, Universal and Graetzin size mantles and a great variety of shades.

Below: *An 1899 advertisement for gas-light fittings.*

Over page: *Tin goods from the 1885 catalogue of Piper, Theobald & Company.*

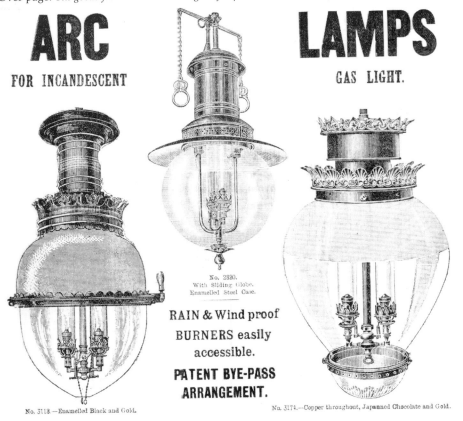

ARC LAMPS

FOR INCANDESCENT

GAS LIGHT.

No. 2380.
With Sliding Globe.
Enamelled Steel Case.

RAIN & Wind proof
BURNERS easily
accessible.

PATENT BYE-PASS
ARRANGEMENT.

No. 3118.—Enamelled Black and Gold.

No. 3174.—Copper throughout, Japanned Chocolate and Gold.

TIN GOODS, BEST QUALITY.

KITCHEN TEAPOTS.
Several Patterns, from 1/10 to 4/6

POTATO PASTY PAN.
9 in. 3/6, 10 in. 4/, 11 in. 5/

WICKER PLATE BASKET.
Tin Lined, 6/6, 8/

BRONCHITIS KETTLE.
4/6

LOYSELL'S COFFEE URN.
In Block Tin and Bronzed Copper, from 12/

PLATE CARRIERS.
Wicker Tin Lined, 13/
Plain Wicker ... 8/6

GAME OVENS, 4/, 5/, 6/
Sausage Toasters, from 1/6
York Ovens   ...   6/

FLOUR DREDGERS.
10d., 1/, 1/2

CHOP COVERS.
8 in. 1/3, 9 in. 1/9

COLANDERS.
Best Planished, 3/, 3/6, 4/
Stamped   ...   1/9, 2/, 2/6
Common, Strong, 9d., 1/, 1/3

JELLY MOULDS, from 1/6 to 7/6

HOT WATER PLATES.
From 2/ to 5/

QUEEN'S CAKE PANS.
4d. each.

FOR FURNISHING LISTS SEE PAGES 61 TO 68.

TIN GOODS, BEST QUALITY.

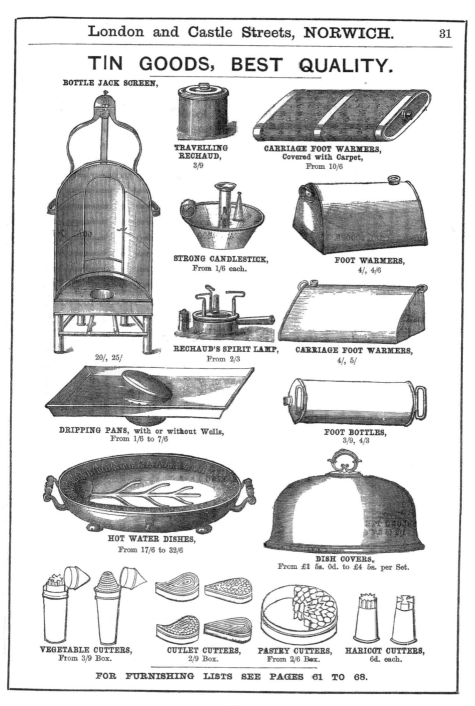

BOTTLE JACK SCREEN,

20/, 25/

TRAVELLING RECHAUD,
3/9

CARRIAGE FOOT WARMERS,
Covered with Carpet,
From 10/6

STRONG CANDLESTICK,
From 1/6 each.

FOOT WARMERS,
4/, 4/6

RECHAUD'S SPIRIT LAMP,
From 2/3

CARRIAGE FOOT WARMERS,
4/, 5/

DRIPPING PANS, with or without Wells,
From 1/6 to 7/6

FOOT BOTTLES,
3/9, 4/3

HOT WATER DISHES,
From 17/6 to 32/6

DISH COVERS,
From £1 5s. 0d. to £4 5s. per Set.

VEGETABLE CUTTERS,
From 3/9 Box.

CUTLET CUTTERS,
2/9 Box.

PASTRY CUTTERS,
From 2/6 Box.

HARICOT CUTTERS,
6d. each.

FOR FURNISHING LISTS SEE PAGES 61 TO 68.

Above left: *The 'Omega' gas heater of 1890.*
Above right: *An early gas stove, the 'Black Beauty', made by R. & A. Main in 1878.*

By the late 1880s he was adding to his established range of petroleum heating stoves, gas heaters and geysers. The stove and grate department flourished in an age of cheap coal; there were fireplaces to be fitted in every room and cookers of every size and description from small cottage ranges to the enormous multi-function ranges for mansions. Grates had to have fenders and fire irons in brass, iron or steel, accessories such as firescreens, fireguards, trivets, bellows and coal scuttles. The drysaltery section supplied Zebra grate polish and Nixey's black lead as well as its essential chemical compounds, gums, candles and often inks, vinegar and treacle!

Almost every item of kitchen equipment was supplied by the ironmonger. Enormous stocks of china and glass were kept and table cutlery was a major item,

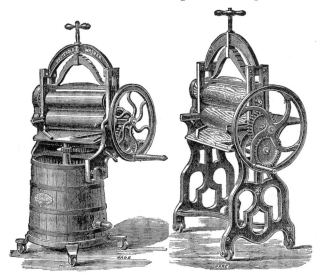

Two of the wide range from Summerscales, 'the largest mangle makers in the world'.

PIPER, THEOBALD & CO.,

SUNDRIES.

Housemaids'
Gloves and Gauntlets,
From 1/ pair.

Plate Baskets,
Wicker, Lined with Baize,
2/9 3/9 4/ 5/6 7/

Mouse Traps, from 1d. to 2/

Hand Bells,
From 1/

Jelly Bag Stands,
From 6/6

Goffering Irons, from 8d. pair.

Beetle Traps, 1/

Strong Vegetable Boilers,
From 2/3

Beer Taps, from 2/

Flat Irons, from 1/ pair.

Brass Adjustable Trivets, 7/9

Patent Corkscrews,
From 1/9

Bright Iron Folding Plate Stand, 19/6

Corkscrews, from 6d,

Table Gongs,
From 1/6 to 7/6

Salamanders, with or without stand, from 5/

FOR FURNISHING LISTS SEE PAGES 61 TO 68.

Various domestic items supplied by Piper, Theobald & Company, including beetle traps and goffering irons.

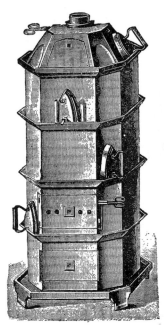

together with electro-plated nickel silver tableware. Before stainless steel began its eventual takeover, the trade sold knife-cleaning boards and machines, thus ensuring a regular trade in knife-cleaning powder.

The cheaper ranges of saucepans, teapots, coffee pots and kettles were made of tinplate, mostly hand-made and varying in quality, 'block tin' being regarded as the best. Tinned copper or copper-bottomed items were better on the iron ranges, and enormous quantities of cast-iron hollow-ware, with tinned or enamelled linings, ultimately predominated, enamelling becoming the most popular finish.

Under the heading 'woodware' in the retailer's catalogue came many items still used today like rolling pins and bread boards, with additions that are now much sought after, like coopered buckets, baths and washtubs, salt and knife boxes. Surprisingly to us, it also included washing machines, mangles and wringers – heavy, cumbersome and exhausting combinations of wood and iron with india-rubber or wooden rollers.

Most of the brushes sold were hand-made of bast, bristle or hair set in pitch, strictly shaped and categorised as to purpose. Patent carpet-sweepers came under this heading as, logically, did doormats.

The ironmonger made random entry to all parts of

Above: *A laundry stove for heating several flat irons simultaneously.*

Below left: *The Excelsior open and close fire from Carron Ironworks, 'especially suitable to stand on boarded floors'.*

Below right: *The Larbert portable kitchen range.*

Open and Close Fire. From 22/6 to 35/-

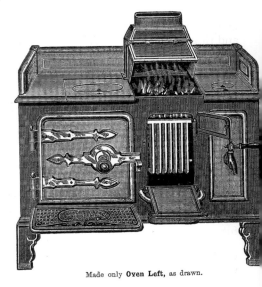

Made only **Oven Left**, as drawn.

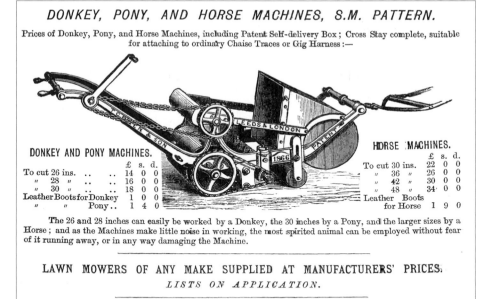

DONKEY, PONY, AND HORSE MACHINES, S.M. PATTERN.

Prices of Donkey, Pony, and Horse Machines, including Patent Self-delivery Box; Cross Stay complete, suitable for attaching to ordinary Chaise Traces or Gig Harness :—

DONKEY AND PONY MACHINES.

	£	s.	d.
To cut 26 ins.	14	0	0
" 28 "	16	0	0
" 30 "	18	0	0
Leather Boots for Donkey	1	0	0
" " Pony ..	1	4	0

HORSE MACHINES.

	£	s.	d.
To cut 30 ins.	22	0	0
" 36 "	26	0	0
" 42 "	30	0	0
" 48 "	34	0	0
Leather Boots for Horse	1	9	0

The 26 and 28 inches can easily be worked by a Donkey, the 30 inches by a Pony, and the larger sizes by a Horse ; and as the Machines make little noise in working, the most spirited animal can be employed without fear of it running away, or in any way damaging the Machine.

LAWN MOWERS OF ANY MAKE SUPPLIED AT MANUFACTURERS' PRICES.
LISTS ON APPLICATION.

Delivered, Carriage Free, at all the principal Railway Stations and Shipping Ports in England, Scotland and Ireland.

Heavy lawn-mowers had to be pulled by donkeys or ponies, specially shod with leather boots to prevent their hooves cutting the turf.

the house with japanned ware ranging from travelling trunks and boxes to buckets, washstands, baths and toilet sets. All sorts of container were decoratively japanned, as were the very popular bird cages, although the best were of brass.

Brass was the metal of the Victorians. It was produced in great quantities for oil lamps, door furniture, fireplace accessories, ornaments, bell fittings, curtain poles and rings and numerous other items. The majority of beds were of brass or iron or both and were sold fully equipped with wire, flock, feather or down mattresses. Ecclesiastical brassware might also be found – candlesticks, crosses and lecterns – and undertakers' supplies like coffin handles, plates and screws. Ironmongers were locksmiths by tradition, and it was natural that fire-proof safes should be added to the stock to safeguard the cash taken by other traders as well as the valuables of the wealthy. A surprising number of safes survived in use for a century or more.

It took some time before the sale of typewriters passed from the ironmonger to the stationer, and it is difficult to imagine where else sports goods would have been sold. Bicycles were welcomed as a new range to sell and service, as were perambulators and pushchairs and ultimately cars. There was an interesting incident when one old-established Suffolk ironmonger (whose business had been founded on the manufacture of long-case clocks) became one of the first agents for the Scottish-made Arrol Johnston motorcar. When he was offered one of the early agencies for the new American Ford he turned it down as he could not see any future for this particular make!

A country ironmonger might have fewer pretensions as a house furnisher but he would need to stock a large range of agricultural items and dairy equipment. A sizable trader would usually have a workshop and foundry geared to the needs of

ELECTRO-PLATED GOODS.

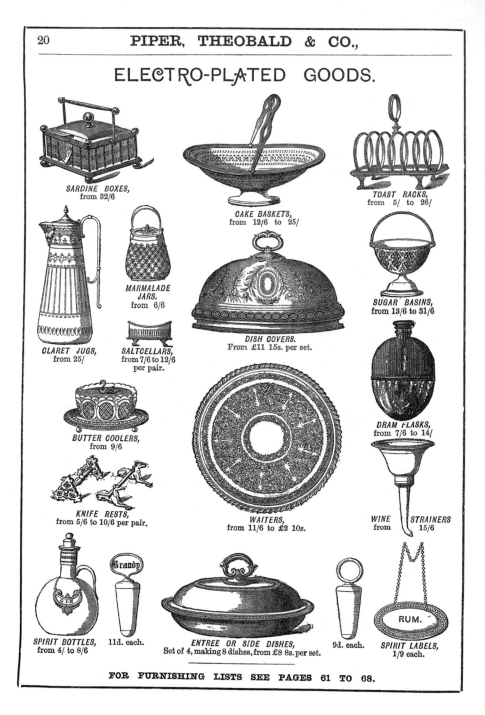

SARDINE BOXES,
from 32/6

CAKE BASKETS,
from 12/6 to 25/

TOAST RACKS,
from 5/ to 26/

MARMALADE
JARS.
from 6/6

DISH COVERS.
From £11 15s. per set.

SUGAR BASINS,
from 13/6 to 31/6

CLARET JUGS,
from 25/

SALTCELLARS,
from 7/6 to 12/6
per pair.

BUTTER COOLERS,
from 9/6

DRAM FLASKS,
from 7/6 to 14/

KNIFE RESTS,
from 5/6 to 10/6 per pair.

WAITERS,
from 11/6 to £2 10s.

WINE STRAINERS
from   15/6

SPIRIT BOTTLES,
from 4/ to 8/6

11d. each.

ENTREE OR SIDE DISHES,
Set of 4, making 8 dishes, from £8 8s. per set.

9d. each.

SPIRIT LABELS,
1/9 each.

RUM.

Brandy

FOR FURNISHING LISTS SEE PAGES 61 TO 68.

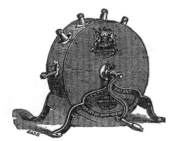

Kent's Patent Knife Cleaners.

To Clean, including Carver.	Colonial.			Kent's Original.			Kent's Improved.			Kent's 1882 Patent.		
	£	s.	d.	£	s.	d.	£	s.	d.	£	s.	d.
3 Knives	1	5	0	1	12	0	2	2	0	2	10	0
4 "	1	15	0	2	10	0	3	3	0	3	10	0
5 "	3	0	0	3	15	0	4	15	0	5	5	0
6 "		...		5	10	0	7	0	0	7	15	0
7 "		...		6	10	0	8	10	0	9	5	0

If on High Stands, from 8/ to 15/ more.

REFRIGERATORS OR PORTABLE ICE HOUSES.

These furnish a Wine Cooler and Provision Safe under one Lock.

	Outside Measurements.			Ordinary.			Ventilated and Improved.		
	W.	D.	H.	£	s.	d.	£	s.	d.
No. 1	22 by 20 by 20		...	3	3	0	...	4 10 0
2	27 by 21 by 30		...	4	4	0	...	5 15 0
3	33 by 22 by 31		...	5	5	0	...	6 15 0
4	39 by 24 by 32		...	6	6	0	...	8 10 0
5	45 by 25 by 33		...	7	7	0	...	9 15 0
6	50 by 27 by 34		...	8	8	0	...	10 15 0

Earthern or Slate Tank with Filter and Plated Taps extra.

Nos. 1, 2 and 3, 20/. Nos. 4, 5 and 6, 25/.

CHEAVIN'S (GOLD MEDAL) RAPID WATER FILTER.

The only Filter which effectually removes Lead, Lime, Iron, Sewage, Organic, Mineral and Saline Impurities, and excels all others in Mechanical and Chemical Action, and is the most effective means known of Purifying Water for Domestic, Manufacturing, and General purposes.

GLASS FILTERS.
From 2/6

6,200 Physicians, Surgeons, and Chemists have these Filters in use.

Nos.	000	00	0	1	2	3	4	5	6
Gallons	½	1½	2½	3½	5	6	7	12	19/
Price of Domestic Filters,	10/6	14/	17/6	25/	35/	42/	50/	70/	90

KNIFE BOARDS.
INDIA RUBBER AND BUFF LEATHER.
From 1/6 to 20/

FOR FURNISHING LISTS SEE PAGES 61 TO 68.

Richmond's 'Gordon' gas fire (above left) and their 'Kitchener' gas cooker from a trade catalogue of 1899.

the farming community: many twentieth-century manufacturers grew out of this department of a rural ironmonger's shop.

The age of the horse demanded a large and varied stock of stable ironmongery and equipment; harness and saddlery were nearly always left to the specialist. Guns were another essential part of rural stock, with cartridges and gunpowder. (An intrepid housewife might buy small quantities of gunpowder to clear the hole in the copper boiler; a small charge in a screw of paper was inserted and set off!) Ropes and twines were always needed, and baskets in a long vanished variety of shapes and sizes, for purposes unknown to us, were stocked. Basket furniture for bedrooms and the garden was a popular line. Cast-iron garden furniture was popular, too, and all garden tools and equipment from rollers and mowers to hoses and tents were stocked.

An advertisement for a horse's name plate taken from the Piper, Theobald & Company catalogue of 1885.

HORSES' NAME PLATES.

For Stalls or Loose Boxes, Suitable for fixing above Manger Fittings.

No. 199.

·KATHLEEN·

16 inches, Japanned any Colour, with Gold Border and Letters ... ... 6s. 6d.

BATHS.

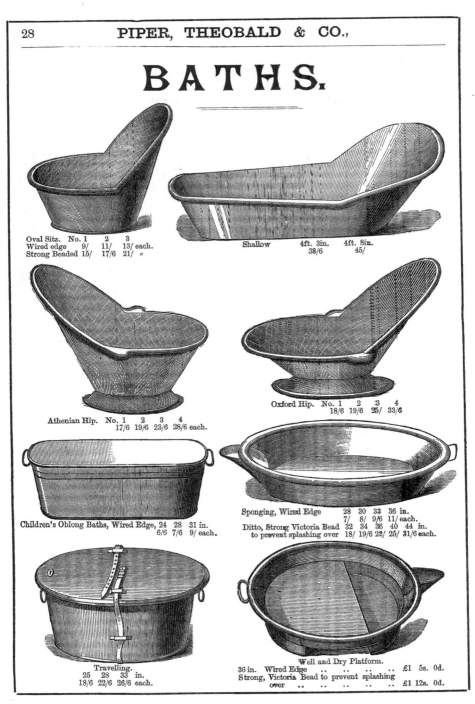

Oval Sitz. No. 1   2   3
Wired edge   9/   11/   13/ each.
Strong Beaded 15/   17/6   21/   "

Shallow   4ft. 3in.   4ft. 8in.
                38/6   45/

Athenian Hip. No. 1   2   3   4
             17/6   19/6   23/6   28/6 each.

Oxford Hip. No. 1   2   3   4
             18/6   19/6   25/   33/6

Children's Oblong Baths, Wired Edge, 24   28   31 in.
                                      6/6   7/6   9/ each.

Sponging, Wired Edge   28   30   33   36 in.
                           7/   8/   9/6   11/ each.
Ditto, Strong Victoria Bead 32   34   36   40   44 in.
to prevent splashing over 18/   19/6   22/   25/   31/6 each.

Travelling.
25   28   33 in.
18/6   22/6   26/6 each.

Well and Dry Platform.
36 in. Wired Edge ..   ..   £1 5s. 0d.
Strong, Victoria Bead to prevent splashing
                over ..   ..   £1 12s. 0d.

In Tring, Hertfordshire, the Grace family established an ironmonger's business in 1750. The photograph above shows the premises in Tring High Street that the business occupied in the 1880s. Later that century it moved along the street to brand new premises shown opposite, with Mrs Emma Grace standing in the doorway. In 2000 G. Grace and Son celebrated 250 years in business and still displays its lion and key trade mark which is visible in both pictures. (Photographs reproduced by courtesy of Gilbert G. Grace.)

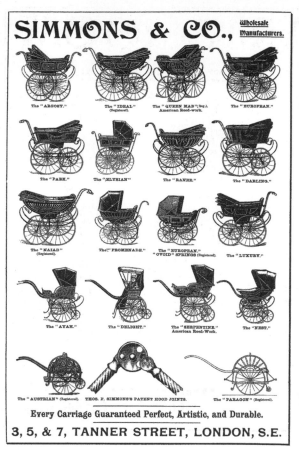

Left: *An advertisement for baby carriages, reproduced from the 'Hardware Trade Journal', 1900.*

Opposite page: *Advertisements from trade journals of the 1890s.*

BYGONES

An alphabetical list of items from a catalogue or stock book of the late nineteenth century yields a great many bygones that are now sought by collectors, interesting either because they are not used or made these days or because they are made differently or in different materials. In a handwritten price book of the 1880s are listed goffering irons for ironing tiny pleats, sad or flat irons to heat on the kitchen range (sharp or rounded ends, in several sizes) and charcoal and box irons, which were heated from inside. Gridirons for grilling over or near the fire and bottle jacks for rotating the roast in front of the fire were still in use. Pestles and mortars were standard items, as well as steel kitchen fenders and irons, bellows, white and black china door furniture, raisin-seeders and cast-iron dumb-bells.

The grocer needed a cheese knife – a large half-moon knife to cut into the huge whole cheese – and the customer used his cheese-taster – a small probe to extract a sample from the piece. The ironmonger supplied him with pewter-type funnels for decanting liquids, wine measures and strainers and vinegar measures. Skid irons, cart and plough traces, frost cogs and screws for carts are on the list.

The prices at which items like these change hands now would astound the owner of the price book.

An ironmonger's shop is the main feature of Halliwell's House Museum, Selkirk, Scotland. The building housed an ironmongery business for almost two hundred years, and the extensive collections of the last owner form the basis of the museum's display.

PLACES TO VISIT

Many museums display items that might have been purchased at a Victorian ironmonger's shop. At each of those listed below, a re-creation of such a shop may be seen. Intending visitors are advised to ascertain the times of opening before making a special journey.

Abbey House Museum, Abbey Walk, Kirkstall, Leeds, West Yorkshire LS5 3EH. Telephone: 0113 230 5492. Website: www.leeds.gov.uk/abbeyhouse
Buckley's Yesterday's World, 89-90 High Street, Battle, East Sussex TN33 0AQ. Telephone: 01424 775378. Website: www.yesterdaysworld.co.uk
Flintham Museum, Inholms Road, Flintham, Newark, Nottinghamshire NG23 5LF. Telephone: 01636 525111.
Halliwell's House Museum, Halliwell's Close, Market Place, Selkirk, Scotland TD7 4BC. Telephone: 01750 20096 or 20054.
'How We Lived Then': Museum of Shops and Local History, 20 Cornfield Terrace, Eastbourne, East Sussex BN21 4NS. Telephone: 01323 737143.
Museum of Lincolnshire Life, The Old Barracks, Burton Road, Lincoln LN1 3LY. Telephone: 01522 528448. Website: www.lincolnshire.gov.uk
The Priest's House Museum, 23-7 High Street, Wimborne Minster, Dorset BH21 1HR. Telephone: 01202 882533. Website: www.priest-house.co.uk
Treadgolds Industrial Heritage Museum, 1 Bishop Street, Portsmouth, Hampshire PO1 3DA. Telephone: 023 928 24745.
Ulster American Folk Park, Mellon Road, Castletown, Omagh, County Tyrone, Northern Ireland BT78 5QY. Telephone: 028 822 43292. Website: www.folkpark.com
York Castle Museum, Eye of York, York YO1 9RY. Telephone: 01904 687687. Website: www.yorkcastlemuseum.org.uk